Table of Contents

Rourke
Educational Media
rourkeeducationalmedia.com

A Division of
Carson Dellosa Education

Can you find these words?

cap

dive

goggles

strokes

Let's Swim!

I am a swimmer.

I am on a swim team.

cap

I wear **goggles**. I wear a **cap**.

I practice swimming with my team.

stroke

We practice our **strokes**.
We practice our kicks.

7

We are ready to race!

We race against other teams.

dive

The whistle blows. I **dive** in the pool. I swim fast.

My teammates swim fast.

Sometimes we win.
Sometimes we lose.

We always have fun!

Did you find these words?

I wear a **cap**.

I **dive** in the pool.

I wear **goggles**.

We practice our **strokes**.

Photo Glossary

 **cap** (kap): A soft, flat hat without a brim.

 **dive** (dive): To go headfirst into water with your arms in front of you.

 **goggles** (GAH-guhlz): Protective glasses that fit tightly around your eyes.

 **strokes** (strohks): Repeated arm movements in swimming.

Index

About the Author

Barry Cole lives in sunny Florida and enjoys living a healthy lifestyle along with his five-year-old son, Brody. His interests include jiu jitsu, running, boating, and anything outdoors.

www.rourkeeducationalmedia.com

PHOTO CREDITS: Cover ©TTStock; Pg 2, 10, 14, 15 ©RyanJLane; Pg 2, 4, 14, 15 ©kali9; Pg 2, 6, 14, 15 ©kali9; Pg 3 ©kali9; Pg 7 ©FatCamera; Pg 8 ©Suzanne Tucker; Pg 9 ©cmcderm1; Pg 11 ©Purdue9394; Pg 12 ©wkali9

Edited by: Kim Thompson
Cover and interior design by: Kathy Walsh

Library of Congress PCN Data
Swimming / Barry Cole
(Ready for Sports)
ISBN 978-1-73160-413-2 (hard cover)(alk. paper)
ISBN 978-1-73160-417-0 (soft cover)
ISBN 978-1-73160-631-0 (e-Book)
ISBN 978-1-73160-654-9 (ePub)
Library of Congress Control Number: 2018967358

CPSIA information can be obtained
at www.ICGtesting.com
Printed in the USA
BVHW022135240522
637339BV00003B/13

9 781731 604170